The Girl And The Dog

Written and illustrated by Deborah Maguire

Copyright 2023 by Three Little Birds Illustration Ltd.
Cloghbally Upper, Co. Cavan, Ireland.

Text and illustrations © Deborah Maguire.

All rights reserved. No part of this book may be reproduced, distributed, or transmitted in any form or by any means, including photocopying, recording or other electronical or mechanical methods, without the prior written permission of the publisher, except in the case of brief quotations embodied in critical reviews and certain other non-commercial uses permitted by copyright law.

All inquiries about this book can be sent to the author at hello@deborahmaguire.ie

First edition published May 2023 by Three Little Birds Illustration Ltd.

For Tadhg, Ruben and George.
Thank you for teaching me so much.

Dear Reader,

This is a story about a girl and her dog. It is a story about friendship, contemplating questions and discovering what matters most.

The girl represents the mind that is curious about the ins and outs of life. She represents a part of me, friends, family, people I've met throughout my life, and I hope, since you are reading this now, you'll find that she represents a part of you too. The dog is wise and calm. He lives in the moment, soaks up all that life has to offer, and through his very existence, has many lessons to share. He is solid, supportive and the most loyal friend (exactly like dogs are!).

These two friends walk every day. Their interactions reflect some important things that the girl learns from the dog. These walks with him enable the girl to think… about big things, small things and everything in between. It's not all about big teachings though. Sometimes, it's just about enjoying the moment shared together… and that perhaps, is the biggest learning of all.

There are two ways you might read this book. You can start at the beginning and read the whole way through to the end. It might be nice to do this one time, so that you can follow them along their walk. Another way to read it is to dip in and out whenever you feel drawn to it. Maybe even close your eyes, flick throught the book, and see which page opens for you.

Whichever way you choose to read this book, I hope you enjoy it,

Deborah

"Why do you love the sunrise?" asked the girl.

"Because it's the start of a brand new day, and anything is possible", said the dog.

"I think it's too steep for me", the girl said worriedly.
"No hill is too steep, just take your time, I'm right beside you."

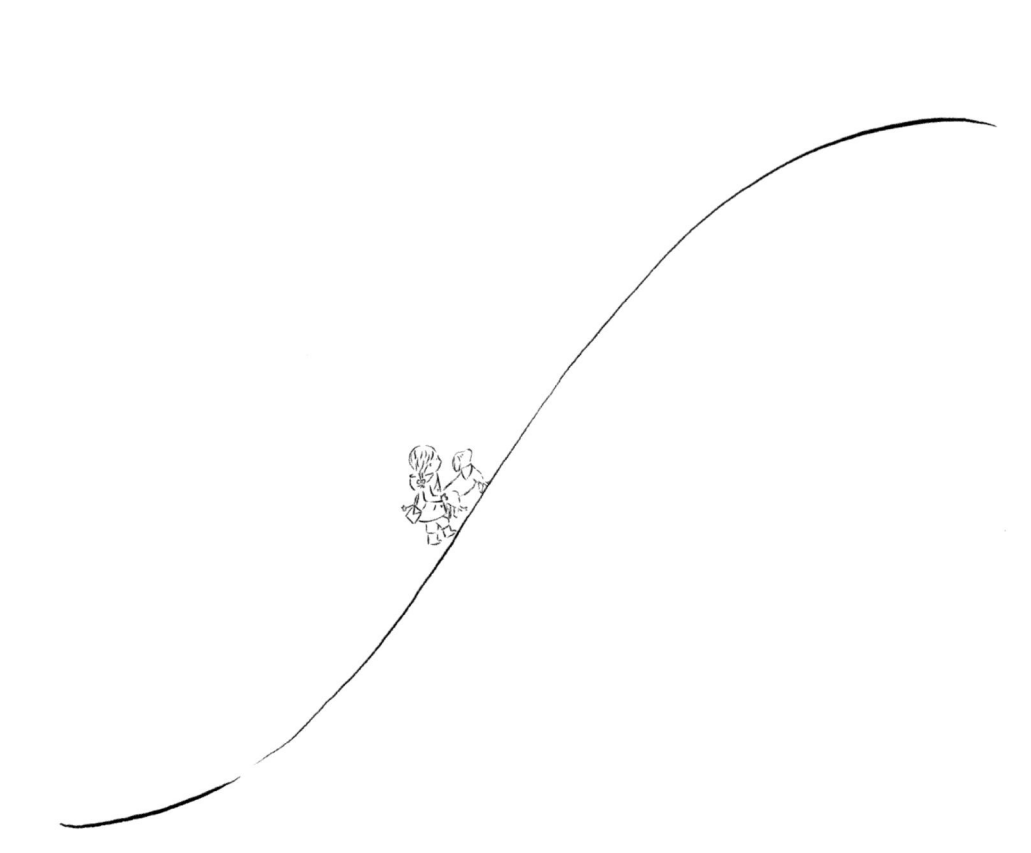

"Always remember how courageous you are."

"Trees are so special. Do you know why?" asked the dog.

"I think we're lost", said the girl.
"Maybe we are at the moment", said the dog, "but we'll find our way".

"It's great to have such a good friend", said the girl.

"What's the hardest thing you've ever done?" asked the girl.

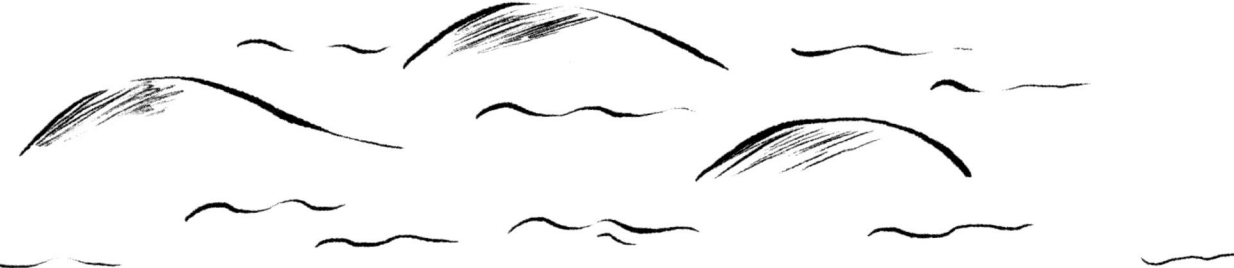

"Believe in myself", said the dog, "but it's also the most important thing I've ever done".

"Isn't it tiny?" said the girl.
"Yes, but sometimes the smallest things are the most important", said the dog.

"Sometimes I feel a little different', said the girl.

"We are all a little different, it's what makes us who we are. On the inside though, we are more alike than we realise", said the dog.

"Would you like some treats?" asked the girl.
"Oh yes please! Treats are always a good idea", said the dog.

"What do you think is the most important thing in the whole wide world?" asked the girl.

"Love", said the dog.

"It's so beautiful", said the girl.
"Thank goodness for that storm", said the dog.

"When the world seems a little upside down, and everything feels scary...

... maybe that's when love matters most"

"Do you ever worry about the future?"
asked the girl.

"Nobody knows what the future will bring", said the dog, "but I do know how lovely today is."

"Why do our hearts feel heavy when we miss someone?" asked the girl.

"It's all the love you hold for them.
It stays with you in your heart", said the dog.

"Being with you makes me happy!"

"Listen!"

"To what?" asked the girl.
"To that", said the dog.
"But there's nothing there, it's just silence", said the girl.
"Exactly... listen to that", said the dog.

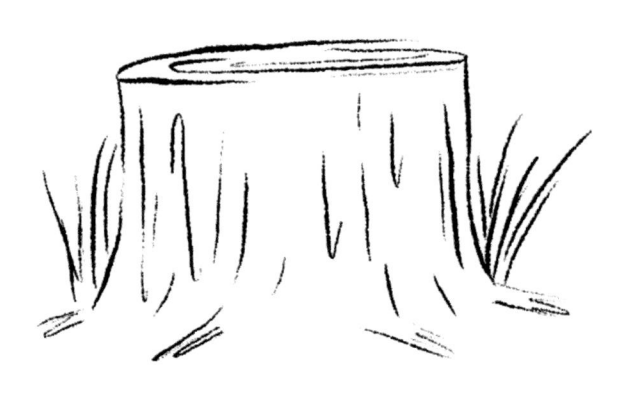

"The moments in between are my favourite", said the dog.

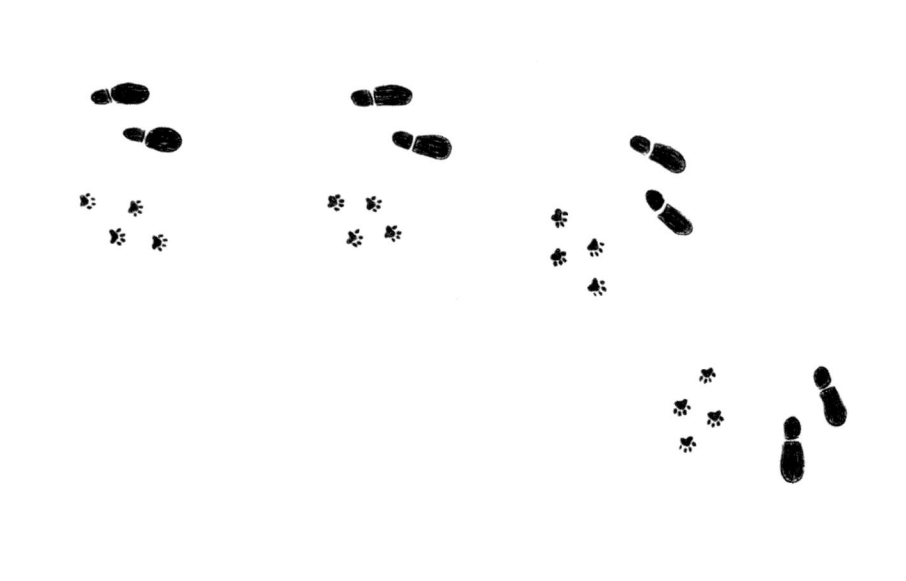

"I think you're wonderful."

"It's getting late, and I can't see as clearly in the dark", said the girl.

"Just put one foot in front of the other, and take your time", said the dog.

"When I'm missing someone, I search the sky for stars", said the girl.
"I do too", said the dog.

"I hear people talking about the little things", said the girl,
"do you know what they are?"
"Oh yes", said the dog.

"They are actually the big things."

"I hope we're always together", said the girl.

"Our hearts will be, forever and ever", said the dog.

Forever

Deborah Maguire is an illustrator and writer, working from her studio, in the Irish countryside. Born in Dublin, she now lives on the border of Meath and Cavan, with her husband, son and dogs.

Deborah loves spending time with her family, being outdoors, books and coffee!

Find her on Instagram
@illustratedbydeborahmaguire
or visit her website
www.deborahmaguire.ie